The CRISIS COUNSELING GUIDEBOOK

Carol Clarke
Virginia Vanderway

Edited by: Dianne Schilling

Copyright © 2011, Innerchoice Publishing • All rights reserved

ISBN – 10: 1-56499-079-2

ISBN – 13: 978-1-56499-079-2

INNERCHOICE Publishing
15079 Oak Chase Court
Wellington, FL 33414

www.InnerchoicePublishing.com

The forms contained in this book may be reproduced in quantities sufficient to ensure effective use in crisis management. All other reproduction by any means or for any purpose whatsoever is explicitly prohibited without written permission. Requests for permission should be directed to INNERCHOICE PUBLISHING.

CONTENTS

CRISIS COUNSELING 7
    What Constitutes a Crisis? 7
    Common Characteristics of Crisis 8
    Types of Crises 8

CRISIS STRATEGIES, INTERVENTIONS AND ACTIVITIES 11

CRISIS INTERVENTION STRATEGIES 13
    Unique Features of Crisis Counseling 13
    Assessment of the Immediate Situation 14
    Your Frame of Mind During and After a Crisis 15
    Tips on Psychological First Aid 16
    When Crisis Counseling Is Needed 17
    Guidelines for Crisis Counseling 17
    Developmental Issues 19
    Reactions to Crises: Developmental Differences 20

CLASSROOM INTERVENTION ACTIVITIES 23
    Preschool and Kindergarten Activities 23
    Elementary School Activities 25
    Additional Strategies for All Ages 28
    Classroom Discussion Guide 32

SELF-CARE, DURING AND AFTER 34
    The Debriefing Meeting 35
    Post Traumatic Stress Disorder 36
    Symptoms of PTSD 37
    Tips for Reducing Post-Crisis Stress 38
    Referral Services 39

DEALING WITH SPECIFIC CRISIS SITUATIONS 43

DEATH AND LOSS 45
Four Psychological Tasks Related to Death for
Children and Adolescents 46
Handling the Class after a Student Dies.. 47
Terminally Ill Students... 48
Responses to Death and Loss 49
Helping Children Through Death and Loss 51
Death Education... 52
Stages of Grieving.. 53
Facing Death: Six Stages 55
After a Death in the Family... 56
Subconcepts About Death That Children Attempt to Understand 58
Developmental Responses to Death, Loss, and Grief........................... 59

SUICIDE 61
Facts about Suicide 61
Social Conditions Associated with Suicide.. 63
Making an Intervention 64
Things to Do 64
Hints for Dealing with a Potential Suicide... 67
Things Not To Do... 68
Determining the Degree of Risk 69
How to Deal with a Suicide 71
Counseling in the Wake of Suicide 73
An Action Plan for Schools 75
Indicators of Potential Teen Suicides 77
Direct Actions of Preventing Suicide 78

NATURAL DISASTERS 79
Feelings/Reactions 80
Dealing with the Feelings/Reactions... 80
Physical Side Effects.. 81
Things to Keep in Mind 82
First Aid Strategies: Earthquake 82
Fear and Anxiety 83
Advice to Parents 84

WAR **85**
    When Parents Are Deployed to a War Zone 85
    Preschool & Kindergarten.. 86
    Elementary School 88

VIOLENCE & GANG DISTURBANCES **91**
    Things to Keep in Mind 91

KIDNAPPING/ABDUCTION.. **95**
    Feelings/General Reactions... 95
    Prevention Strategies... 95
    Issues and Points to Keep in Mind 96

TERRORIST/HOSTAGE SITUATIONS **97**
    Feelings/Reactions and Hints for Dealing with Them 98
    Things to Keep in Mind 99

HOW PARENTS CAN HELP IN A CRISIS **101**
    Following a Crisis, Some Children May: 101
    Ways Parents Can Help Their Children 103

FORMS AND SAMPLE LETTERS **105**

ABOUT THE AUTHORS **117**

CRISIS COUNSELING

What Constitutes a Crisis?

Crises are often sudden, unanticipated events that profoundly and negatively affect a significant segment of the school population. Serious injury and death are common precursors of crisis. However, any intolerable situation, unstable condition, or sudden change in routine that requires immediate attention and resolution can also signal a crisis for the individuals involved. An event that is perceived as emotionally or physically threatening and leads children or adults to believe that they have lost control and are unable to cope is unquestionably a crisis for those individuals.

Common Characteristics of Crisis

Generally, crises consist of abnormal, uncommon and extraordinary conditions that bring forth strong emotional reactions, such as high levels of fear, stress, disequilibrium, and anger, along with an unusually high number of negative confrontations.

A crisis has the potential to upset the entire school community and may be so traumatic that it alters the consciousness of schools and communities for years to come.

In all crises, the immediate needs of people must be identified and addressed to resolve the situation. Immediate needs in a crisis situation usually involve issues of physical welfare, emotional stability, and personal security.

Types of Crises

Abnormal, uncommon and extraordinary conditions are regularly wrought by nature. Following an earthquake in northern California, school children were terrorized by a door slamming or the jiggling of a desk as the earth signaled its settling with hundreds of aftershocks. After a hurricane ravaged the Louisiana coast, sad, hyperactive, depressed, and angry students trickled back to damaged schools over a period of weeks and sometimes months. Many, their homes destroyed, lived in shelters.

Very little if anything can be done to prevent natural disasters, and we seem increasingly ill equipped to predict, much less head off, the violent acts of individuals.

No one noticed when a disenchanted student strolled down the quiet middle school hallway armed with a semiautomatic weapon, entered his math class and calmly killed the teacher and two students, and seriously injured a third. On the other hand, a number of neighbors, friends, and school officials were familiar with the violent nature of the troubled teenager who bludgeoned to death his parents, grandparents and 10-year-old sister, but psychologists counseling the little girl's classmates were no doubt hard pressed to explain how his heinous behavior might have been prevented.

Economic events can precipitate crises, too. When thousands of teachers in a large school district went on strike, children responded with confusion, guilt and tears at seeing their beloved teachers walking noisy picket lines while strangers took over their classrooms.

Here is a partial list of the types of events and conditions that can lead to school crisis:

Natural
- hurricanes
- earthquakes
- tornadoes
- floods
- fires

Environmental
- industrial accidents
- chemical leaks
- nuclear incidents

Economic
- sudden widespread unemployment
- industrial closings
- bank failures
- employee strikes

Social
- tragic deaths
- violent assaults
- homicides
- suicides
- fatal accidents
- serious contagious illness
- crimes
- imprisonments
- acts of sexual deviance
- war

The purpose of crisis counseling is to help children and staff deal with the emotions and reactions aroused by a crisis situation while facilitating a return to normal school operations. This guide has been prepared to assist counselors with appropriate and helpful interventions to employ in responding to a crisis situation and with specific guidance for dealing with identified crises as they emerge.

CRISIS STRATEGIES, INTERVENTIONS AND ACTIVITIES

CRISIS INTERVENTION STRATEGIES

Unique Features of Crisis Counseling

Crisis counseling differs from other forms of counseling in several important ways. The primary goal in crisis counseling is to restore the student to equilibrium. As a result, crisis counseling is more limited in scope and briefer in duration than most other forms of counseling. Other differences are:

- In traditional counseling an effort is made to avoid creating dependency on the counselor. In crisis counseling, temporary dependency is often encouraged and may be necessary to help a student get beyond the initial devastation of the incident.

- In traditional counseling, the student does a lot of talking and the counselor does a lot of listening. The crisis counselor listens too, but is typically more proactive — giving information and advice, making suggestions, offering coping strategies and, if necessary, being highly directive.

- Crisis counseling carries a far greater potential for breach of confidentiality, particularly in cases where students may be a danger to themselves or others, or where school policy or the law require immediate reporting of specific kinds of incidents or behaviors.

Assessment of the Immediate Situation

Emergency situations often trigger crises, the two are not synonymous. School-wide emergencies such as a shooting or a devastating earthquake may not be particularly threatening to some students. Others, though threatened, will be able to cope. Still others will experience extreme trauma.

When an emergency situation occurs, immediately direct attention toward defusing the potential hazard and helping people cope with it. Quickly mobilize appropriate physical and interpersonal resources, and attempt to foster social support and communication among members of the school community. Provide accurate information about the hazard and show students and staff appropriate coping strategies — individually, in small groups, or class by class. Throughout this process, attempt to identify those already in crisis or at high risk and extend them special attention.

Important Things to Keep in Mind During and After a Crisis

- Accept every person's right to his or her own feelings. Remember that reactions can be different because perceptions of the experience differ. Do not place a judgment on feelings shared. Right or wrong — it is a feeling. LISTEN!

- Accept a person's limitations. People who have gone through a traumatic experience need time to recover.

- Size up a distressed person's abilities and concerns as accurately and quickly as possible. Use your counseling skills.

- Accept your own limitations in a relief role. Know yourself well. Remember, you cannot do everything and your own past experiences may get in the way.

People in crisis need help and they need it right away. Intervene immediately with *psychological first aid*. The longer a person remains in a situation of confusion, the greater the resulting anxiety and pain.

Crisis first aid is designed to reestablish immediate coping, not as a final resolution of the crisis. It involves immediate on-the-spot assistance. Its goals are to provide support, reduce emotional damage, and connect the person with other helping resources. Psychological first aid addresses immediate concerns and needs.

Tips on Psychological First Aid

- Provide immediate, direct, active, authoritative intervention.
- Recognize that people in crisis are in a temporary state of disturbance, not mentally ill.
- Communicate confidence in yourself.
- Communicate in a calm, organized way; help limit disorganization and confusion.
- Provide accurate information about the situation. Answer questions.
- Accept every person's right to his or her own feelings.
- Attempt to calm the victim and relieve anxiety and stress, but do not make unrealistic promises.
- Accept a person's limitations as real.
- Do not immediately impose your methods of problem solving upon a disaster victim; in most instances the person's own solutions will be more successful.
- Listen actively.
- Accept your own limitation in a relief role; do not attempt to be all things to all people.

When Crisis Counseling Is Needed

For students who need or desire more than "first aid," attention shifts to providing continued assistance in handling and resolving the crisis situation.

The purpose of extended crisis counseling is to help students realize a final resolution of the crisis by working through all aspects of the experience until they have achieved mastery over it. Carefully evaluate both the student's needs and your own professional skills and competencies before assuming responsibility for longer term crisis counseling. When the demands of the situation fall outside the scope of your abilities, refer.

If your school is in an area where abundant qualified professional referral services are available, you will probably be able to refer most crises situations. If few outside resources are available, you will need to be prepared to handle more situations internally.

Guidelines for Crisis Counseling

Give information about what is normal. When students understand the range of reactions that people often have in crisis situations, their feelings and experiences become more comprehensible and less threatening to them, and they realize that they are normal.

Be concerned and competent. Give the student reassurance and present yourself as a model of competent problem solving. Demonstrate the process of gathering information, choosing between alternatives, and taking action.

Actively listen to the facts of the situation.
Carefully gather information about the crisis, including details about the student's involvement and/or reactions. Concrete knowledge of the situation will shed light on whether the client is behaving rationally or irrationally, allowing you to proceed accordingly.

Listen to and reflect the student's feelings.
Explicitly focus discussion on the student's affect and encourage its expression. Listening to feelings shows empathy, builds rapport and facilitates understanding; it also lets the student know that feelings can be discussed and are part of problem solving.

Help the student accept that a crisis situation has occurred. Denial and defensiveness prolong the crisis situation and prevent mastery of it.

Do not encourage or support blaming. Blaming is basically a waste of time. As long as the student's energy is focused on finding someone to blame for the situation, mastery and responsible problem solving cannot occur.

Do not give false reassurance. Be truthful and realistic. A student in crisis is overwhelmed by powerful emotions — anxiety, tension, anger, depression. Acknowledge that these feelings, and the student's memory of the crisis, may never entirely go away. At the same time, build hope that the situation can start improving right away.

Encourage the student to take action. In every meeting or session, specify some action that the student is able and willing to take. The more a student takes the role of actor, the less he or she will remain in the role of victim.

Facilitate the workings of the student's support network. Encourage the child to solicit and accept help from friends and family.

Engage in focused problem solving. Once you and the student have completely defined the problem — including all sources of concern — brainstorm alternatives and help the student develop a course of action.

Build the student's self-concept. A student in crisis is likely to feel powerless and out of control. As counseling progresses, reinforce each millimeter of movement, emphasizing the student's role as the architect of change.

Encourage self-reliance. As the goals of counseling are met — dealing with feelings, achieving mastery of the event, and problem solving — the disturbing effects of the crisis will diminish, allowing the student to gradually regain psychological independence and autonomy.

Developmental Issues

It will come as no surprise that a child of six and a teenager of sixteen have different cognitive, emotional, and social skills for dealing with crisis. You will want to vary your counseling approaches and techniques accordingly. The charts on the next two pages show expected reactions to crisis at different age levels. They were developed by Scott Poland, a nationally recognized expert on school crisis.

In general, younger students have greater difficulty acknowledging a crisis and are more prone to deny its occurrence. In counseling children, more time is spent exploring reactions and feelings and establishing support systems than on problem solving. Counseling often involves the use of nonverbal activities, such as drawing a picture to express feelings or using music to express thoughts and emotions. Children with some writing ability benefit from completing sentence starters related to the crisis.

Older children and adolescents respond well to verbal exploration of feelings and options, and on focused problem solving.

Reactions to Crises: Developmental Differences

Childhood Reactions to Disaster

- Fear of future disasters
- Loss of interest in school
- Regressive behaviors
- Sleep disturbances and night terrors

Preschool Reactions

- Thumb sucking
- Bed wetting
- Clinging to parents
- Fear of the dark and animals
- Sleep disturbances
- Speech problems
- Loss of appetite
- Toileting regression

(Continued Next Page)

Reactions to Crises: Developmental Differences (Cont.)

Reactions: Ages 5-11

- Irritability
- Whining and clinging behavior
- Aggressive behavior
- More competition with siblings
- Night terrors; nightmares
- School avoidance
- Withdrawal from peers
- Concentration problems

Reactions: Ages 11-14

- Sleep disturbance
- Appetite disturbance
- Rebellion at home
- School problems
- Somatic complaints
- Decreased peer socialization

Reactions: Ages 14-18

- Somatic complaints
- Appetite/sleep problems
- Agitation or decreased energy level
- Less interest in opposite sex
- Irresponsible or delinquent problems
- Concentration problems

CLASSROOM INTERVENTION ACTIVITIES

When working with children in any setting, including the classroom, give them permission to experience a range of emotions. A child stating that she doesn't care today may cry tomorrow. Insist that the children give the same latitude to one another.

When a classmate dies, do not rush to remove the desk and personal possessions of the deceased. Involve students in that process. Ask, "What do you think we should do with John's desk?" Encourage the students to contact the family of the deceased in person or through cards and letters.

If possible, have a school psychologist follow the class schedule of a deceased student on the day that the death is announced. The psychologist can assist in leading discussion and activities, such as those that follow.

Preschool and Kindergarten Activities

Play Reenactment

Use toys — fire trucks, rescue trucks, dump trucks, ambulances, building blocks, dolls, etc. — to encourage the children to reenact their experiences and observations during the traumatic event. Play enactment can help the children to integrate difficult experiences.

Physical Contact

Children need a lot of physical contact during times of stress to help regain a sense of security. Games that involve structured (controlled) physical touching are helpful in this regard.

Nourishment

Having on hand extra amounts of finger foods and fluids is a concrete way of providing the emotional and physical nourishment children need in times of stress. Oral satisfaction is especially necessary as children tend to revert to more regressive or primitive behavior in response to feelings that their survival or security is threatened.

Puppets

Play with puppets can be effective in reducing inhibitions and encouraging children to verbalize feelings.

Art

Have the children do a mural on butcher paper using topics, such as "What happened when..." Do this in small groups, with an adult leading discussion afterwards. Have the children draw individual pictures about the event and then discuss or act out elements of their pictures in small groups. This activity allows children to vent their feelings and assists them to discover that others share their fears.

Stories

Read stories to the children that tell about the experiences of nonfictional children or fictional children and animals in disastrous events. Stories are a nonthreatening vehicle for conveying common reactions to frightening experiences. They are also an excellent way to stimulate discussion. Emphasize how the characters in the stories resolved their feelings of fear.

Large Muscle Activity

When the children are restless or anxious, any activities that involve large muscle movements are helpful. Try skipping, jumping, stretching, or your own simple version of "Jazzercise" (exercises to music).

Elementary School Activities

Play Reenactment

Use toys — fire trucks, rescue trucks, dump trucks, ambulances, building blocks, dolls, etc. — to encourage the children to reenact their experiences and observations during the traumatic event. Play reenactment can help the children to integrate difficult experiences.

Puppets

Play with puppets can be effective in reducing inhibitions and encouraging children to talk about their feelings and thoughts. Children will often respond more freely to a puppet asking about what happened than to an adult asking the questions directly. Help or encourage the children to develop skits or puppet shows about the traumatic event. Encourage them to include anything positive about the experience as well as those aspects that were frightening or disconcerting.

Art and Discussion Groups

Do a group mural on butcher paper with topics such as "What happened in your neighborhood (school, home) when..." This activity is recommended for small groups with discussion afterward, facilitated by an adult, and can help the children vent their feelings and feel less alone with their fears. Have the children draw individual pictures and then talk about them in small groups. Always try to end group discussion on a positive note, for example by encouraging a feeling of mastery or preparedness. In addition to providing students with an opportunity to talk about their feelings, emphasize how the community or family pulled together to deal with the crisis.

Share Your Own Experience

Stimulate group discussion about disaster experiences by sharing your own feelings, fears or experiences. It is very important to legitimize tumultuous feelings as a way of helping children feel less isolated.

Disaster Plans

Have the children brainstorm their own classroom or family disaster plan. What would they do if they had to evacuate? How would they contact parents? How should the family be prepared? How could they help the family?

Reading

Read aloud or have the children read stories or books that talk about children or families dealing with stressful situations, pulling together during times of hardship, etc.

Creative Writing or Discussion Topics

Have the children describe in detail "A very scary intense moment" or "A very happy moment." Create a group story, recorded by the teacher, about a dog or cat that is in an earthquake or flood. What happens to him? What does he do? How does he feel. You can help the students by providing connective elements. Emphasize creative problem solving and creating a positive resolution.

Playacting

In small groups play the game, "If you were an animal, what would you be?" You might adapt discussion questions such as, "If you were that animal, what would you do when...?" Have the children take turns acting out an emotion in front of the class (without talking) and have the rest of the class guess what the feeling is and why the actor has that feeling. (Act out positive as well as negative feelings.)

Other Disasters

Have the students bring in newspaper clippings on disasters that have happened in other parts of the world. Ask them to imagine how the survivors might have felt or what they might have experienced. In discussion, invite them to answer the question, "Have you ever had a similar experience or feeling?"

Tension Breakers

"Co-listening" is a good tension breaker when the children are restless. Have the children quickly pair up with a partner. Child #1 takes a turn talking about anything he or she wants to, while child #2 simply listens. After three minutes they switch roles and # 2 talks while #1 listens.

When the children are anxious and restless, any activities that involve large muscle movements are helpful. Skip, jump, stretch, or do your own version of "Jazzercise" (exercises to music).

Additional Strategies for All Ages

The following strategies are adapted from *Family Life Education, Consulting, Program Development Seminars* by Margaret Wolf, and are temporary aids for restoring calmness in a disaster.

Wind the Clock

The first moments of an emergency situation are often the time when a psychological choice is made between panic and control. Airplane pilots are taught to engage in a commonplace activity, such as winding their wristwatch, in order to "ground" their thoughts. The gesture or action can be anything, — clapping hands, tapping nose, unbuttoning and rebuttoning a shirt button, etc. The objective is to perform a predetermined action that will trigger thoughts of calmness.

Deep Breathing

Inhale, hold and exhale to the count of 4, 6 and then 10. In moments of panic, heart and breathing rates rapidly increase. Controlling the breath calms the heart and emotions. Have students do 5 repetitions at each level, increasing the breath count as calmness sets in. Deep breathing is best done with closed eyes so that unpleasant visual stimuli do not distract concentration.

Singing

Use songs that everyone recognizes such as Christmas Carols. Feelings are right brain responses. Singing, because of it's creative component, is also a right brain function. (Talking, logic, and reason are left brain functions.) By substituting a controlled right brain activity, such as singing, for a detrimental emotional response, you can temporarily bring emotions under control.

Creative Visualization

Guide a group of students through an imagery that is peaceful. Guided imagery should begin with a few minutes of deep breathing. The leader then talks the group through the visualization, incorporating many sensory recollections. Example: *Imagine you are going to the beach. It is a beautiful, warm day and, as you get out of the car at the beach, you are immediately struck by the smell of the suntan oil and water. Feel the warm sand under your feet as you walk through the crowds of people to your favorite spot. The air is warm and a gust of wind blows your hair about as you spread your towel out on the warm sand. You sink into the towel and you are aware of how comforting the warmth of the sun feels on your body. Feel the sun right now as it cloaks your whole body in comfort. (Pause for 10 seconds.) Now you are aware of the sound of the surf as it flows back and forth across the shore. Listen and watch the surf for a few minutes, concentrating on the sounds of the waves as they flow back and forth. (Pause for a minute.) Now it is time to leave the beach. Sit up and take a last look at the ocean, relishing the calmness and peace you have felt here. As you pack up your towel and walk back to the car, you are grateful, knowing that you can come back to this special place in your mind any time you want to. (Pause 10 seconds) When you feel ready, open your eyes.*

Group Rap Sessions

Allow participants to express their feelings and to recognize that others share their fears and concerns. You might begin by offering a sentence starter or topic, such as "The thing that surprised me the most was…" or "What concerns me the most now is…" Allow all those who wish to comment an opportunity to do so. This kind of structure helps to keep the emotional content focused. This is not a format for uncontrolled emotional expression. Hysteria is catching. If someone is panicked, remove that person from the group until he or she has calmed down. It is important not to talk students out of their feelings. "I understand how you feel," or "That must be very hard for you," acknowledges the person's feelings without judgment.

Encourage Constructive Physical Activity

Physical activity channels emotional energy in a positive direction. This helps to discharge the emotional energy as well as to create camaraderie and the sense of doing something to solve the problem at hand.

Creative Writing and Artistic Experiences

Use these strategies to help older children to vent their feelings and concerns. The activity should be somewhat structured. For example, direct the students to: "Write about the heroic acts you witnessed," or "Write about your experiences first in journal form and then as if you were a newspaper reporter observing the experience." The latter approach allows students to approach the subject more objectively and impersonally.

Classroom Discussion Guide

The following list provides guidelines for classroom discussions related to a school crisis. Following announcement of a crisis situation, use the open-ended questions (or similar questions that you develop) to facilitate discussion.

1. Review the facts and dispel rumors.
2. If a suicide occurs, discuss facts and myths about suicide.
3. Inform students of locations for grief support.
4. Encourage students to express their reactions in a way that is appropriate for them, and affirm the appropriateness of all responses from severe upset to no visible reactions whatsoever.
5. Discuss possible guilt feelings or feelings of responsibility.
6. Discuss students' possible fears for their safety and that of their peers and siblings.
7. Ask students to support one another and to escort any friend who needs additional help to one of the designated locations for grief support.
8. Reassure students that any adult in the building is available to help.
9. Allow students to discuss other losses they have experienced. Help them understand that this loss may bring up past losses; this is normal.
10. Encourage students to discuss their feelings with their parents/families.

(Continued Next Page)

Classroom Discussion Guide (Cont.)

Questions:

1. What was it like for you when you heard the news?

2. Did/will you discuss it at home? How did it go? How do you think it will go?

3. If you were a member of _____'s family, what do you think you would want at a time like this?

4. How can you students help each other through this?

5. What other losses have you experienced?

6. What thoughts and feelings does this bring up for you?

Reproduced from Preventing Chaos in Times of Crisis,
Southwest Regional Laboratory, Los Alomitos, California, 1992

SELF-CARE, DURING AND AFTER

Some counselors may have a tendency to become so intent (and intense) in their efforts to help others that they will forget to pay attention to their own physical and emotional needs. Many will forego breaks and forget to eat. Others will forget completely about routine contacts they make with family members throughout the day. Some will even put off going home at night or, if they do go, have difficulty sleeping.

Begin to emphasize self-care for counselors and other staff as soon as possible after a crisis event, and continue to do so routinely. Support and monitor each other, share stress-management strategies, and treat self-care like a discipline until it becomes a habit.

When the crisis ends, don't attack the accumulated work as if you could get it all done in a day. Remember you have been in a traumatic situation. Pace yourself. Give yourself time to recharge. If you take care of yourself each time you'll be more able to handle the next demanding issue. If you are not careful, unrelieved stress will take it's toll. So DO TAKE CARE OF YOURSELF, and remind your staff to do the same.

The Debriefing Meeting

Crisis counselors, like the students and staff, need time to tell their trauma story — to ventilate, receive group support, begin their own grieving process, do an exercise or two to reduce stress, and pay attention to symptoms of Post Traumatic Stress Disorder (PTSD) in themselves and other staff members. If necessary, counselors should have an opportunity to be assessed by an outside professional. This process can begin in a debriefing meeting.

The crisis debriefing meeting is a time-limited focused group in which counselors and other staff members and support personnel review the factual events of the day; share their feelings, thoughts, and physical reactions; discuss what worked, what didn't and why; and plan follow-up tasks and procedures. As part of the meeting, participants should be reminded to watch for personal and work-performance changes that signal post-traumatic stress.

When a crisis incident has been extremely severe, it might be wise to ask a mental health professional trained in crisis intervention and PTSD to lead the meeting. Someone from a trusted referral agency would be a logical choice.

Post Traumatic Stress Disorder

After a traumatic event has been experienced, survived, and completed, it is not uncommon to experience "aftershocks" — strong emotional and physical reactions that appear a few hours, days, or weeks later. These reactions can last from six to eight weeks and, in some cases, longer. They are normal; however, they don't *feel* normal and can be alarming to the person experiencing them, as well as to family and friends. Occasionally, professional help is required to successfully manage symptoms during this difficult period.

Symptoms of PTSD

- Re-experiencing the event
- uncontrollable intrusive thoughts
- anticipation of repetition
- anxiety
- re-experiencing the same bodily state or physical symptoms initially experienced at the time of the event
- vulnerable to minimal stress
- blunting of affect
- intense fear, helplessness, loss of control
- rage
- depression with or without agitation
- impulsive behavior
- explosive episodes
- flashbacks
- restlessness
- sleep disturbances
- physical complaints
- avoidance of activities which recall the event
- self-destructive behavior
- suicide ruminations
- self-medication/substance abuse
- sense of loss

Tips for Reducing Post-Crisis Stress

- Exercise. Take a long walk, preferably with a friend.
- Start a new routine or hobby.
- Bring order to something as a way of combatting your sense of helplessness. Organize something, like a closet or a room.
- Listen to music.
- Seek the peace and serenity of nature.
- Talk to someone who loves you.
- Meditate. Practice deep breathing exercises or guided visualization.
- Write thank-you letters.
- Take a bubble bath or relax in a jacuzzi.
- Watch an uplifting movie.
- Regain your perspective by reading something humorous and insightful — like a collection of "Calvin and Hobbs."

Referral Services

Your school district may already have a community resource publication that includes the types of help listed below. If you do not have such a guide, it is extremely important that you develop one. The following format may be used as an example of telephone numbers you'll want to have at hand.

Phone numbers by themselves, however, are not enough. Your list should also contain the name of the agency or provider and a contact person prepared to work with the school during a crisis.

Death
- Organizations for parents whose children have died
- Hospice organizations

Gangs
- Gang prevention/intervention groups
- Police department gang prevention detail

Hostage Situations
- Emergency Police/Fire
- Crisis hotline

Abduction
- Child Quest International (408) 287-4673
  www.childquest.org
- Find the Children (888)477-6721
  www.findthechildren.com
- National Center for Missing and Exploited Children 24-hour hotline (800) The Lost (843-5678)
  www.missingkids.com

Natural Disaster
- Red Cross
- Shelter/housing
- Food/clothing
- Child protective services
- Emergency family assistance
- Disaster relief
- Medical

Rape
- Child protective services
- Rape crisis centers
- Rape hotlines

Suicide
- Suicide prevention groups
- Suicide hotlines
- Survivors of suicide support groups

Molestation
- Police
- Sexual assault support groups
- Child protective services

General Counseling Services
- Child
- Family
- Alcohol and other drugs
- Post Traumatic Stress Disorder

Health Services and Clinics
- Medical and dental
- Hospital — medical
- Hospital — psychiatric

Other Hotlines
- Crisis
- Sexual abuse
- Other community hotlines

Self-help Groups
- Alcoholics Anonymous
- Al-Anon/Alateen
- Parent support
- Other self-help groups

Law Enforcement
- Police or sheriff
- Probation

Social Services and Child Welfare
- Department of children's services
- Department of mental health
- Other departments

Bilingual/Bicultural Resources
- Translators
- Agencies and programs

DEALING WITH SPECIFIC CRISIS SITUATIONS

DEATH AND LOSS

Immediately upon receiving the news of the pupil's (or teacher's) death, schedule a meeting with the principal, teachers involved, and a school counselor or psychologist to discuss how to deal with the situation, including the reactions of peers and parents.

Designate one or more of those present to discuss the death with the pupil's classmates and to answer questions. If the person who knows the class best, the teacher, is not prepared to handle the session, ask him or her to be present while another person (principal, school counselor, psychologist or other appropriate personnel) leads the discussion.

Outgrowths of the class discussion may include:

1. a plan of action for removal of the deceased pupil's belongings;
2. sending a message of condolence to the family; and
3. some sort of memorial for the deceased student/teacher.

Ideally, the students should have considerable input into the design of the plan. The students will let you know when they feel the discussion and related activities are complete.

In the immediate aftermath of these activities, the teacher should respond to individual and group requests to talk about death, either in general or in relation to the deceased student. Discussions about death can be important learning experiences for students. At the same time, they provide opportunities for the teacher to observe the progress of students in resolving the loss.

The principal and/or school counselor should continue to follow up with the teacher to check on how the class is progressing, to resolve any issues concerning further contact with the family of the deceased, and to identify effects that the death has had on classroom activity.

Four Psychological Tasks Related to Death for Children and Adolescents

1. Understanding death in general and in specific situations. The best explanation may be, "Death is when the body stops working."

2. Dealing with their own feelings, including sadness, anger, and guilt. This can take many months.

3. Finding an appropriate way to remember the person who died.

4. Going on. Frequently, after understanding, grieving, and commemorating, a child needs permission from adults to "go on."

Handling the Class after a Student Dies

Almost all teachers touched by a death in the classroom or the school community need help in handling their classes. The following strategies, which involve many sharing experiences, will help:

1. Don't be impassive about a student's death. Share reactions with the class.
2. Let the children talk and write about their feelings.
3. Listen to whatever students have to say. Never shut off discussion.
4. Speak honestly and directly about the circumstances under which the student died. Avoid euphemistic language. Make a clear distinction between the illness of a child who dies and any medical problems his or her classmates experience. This is especially important with your students.
5. Never tell young children, "God took Sally away because He loves her." Children will wonder if it's a good idea to be loved by God. Likewise, don't say, "Sally went to sleep." You may create a class of insomniacs.
6. Don't force a "regular day" upon grieving students, but at the same time, don't allow the class to be totally unstructured. Offer choices of activities, such as letters, journals, and discussions.
7. Suggest that the students write personal sympathy notes to the parents of a deceased classmate, or to any student who has suffered a loss. See they are delivered to the appropriate people after careful screening.
8. Older students may want to plan more concrete expressions of concern. Allow them to arrange a schedule for making food, such as casseroles and

desserts. Help them raise money for a memorial scholarship fund, medical research donations, or a cause especially commemorative of the deceased student.
9. Make sure that visitation times are well publicized, perhaps with a tactful lesson on funeral etiquette.
10. Explain how students should treat a bereaved student who is returning to school. Emphasize that trying to avoid the student, or being overly solicitous, will not help. Point out the need to resume normal relationships.
11. Remember that your class could remain quiet and depressed for some time after a death, and that some students may begin to act out noisily and physically as a way of letting adults know they are struggling with their feelings..

Terminally Ill Students

Increasingly, school personnel must deal with terminally ill students. Schooling is vital for dying children because it helps to maintain their self-image. Besides, it assures students that parents and teachers have faith in their future.

To cope effectively, school personnel should be aware that dying students have certain basic needs. They need to:

- know that they are dying
- experience meaningful communication
- live to the end with dignity
- be listened to without anger and with acceptance
- have hope
- know that they are valuable individuals
- know that they are not forgotten
- maintain self-esteem

RESPONSES TO DEATH AND LOSS

Feelings/Reactions	Strategies for Helpers
• Disbelief, shock, apathy daydreaming	• Give them opportunities to talk about their thoughts and feelings; get accurate information as soon as possible.
• Drop in school performance	• Use sensitivity in maintaining status quo.
• Fear that someone they love may be lost	• Explore this possibility and allow them to express this fear. Encourage other adults to be open and honest about their own feelings.
• Misunderstandings about causes and meaning of death/loss	• Encourage a review of pleasant and unpleasant memories of the deceased. Allow for catharsis, confession, remembrance and release.
• Guilt feelings that something they did or didn't do has caused the death/loss	• Allow the students to talk about it. Do not reassure too quickly.
• Anger	• Allow it to be expressed verbally without overreacting. It is a natural part of the grieving process. Allow some time for sorting out, but keep giving opportunities for verbalizing.
• Coping and surviving	• Establish positive direction and assistance.

Here are some specific things that teachers and other school personnel can do when dealing with a terminally ill student:

1. Read about the disease, and facilitate classroom discussion that can foster social acceptance.

2. Contact health personnel, parents and professionals who have worked with the student in the past to find out the best ways to meet physical and health needs.

3. Modify the instructional program to accommodate fatigue, excessive absences and the effects of medication.

4. Reduce instructional goals so that some goals can be completed, giving the student feelings of success.

5. Do not make the student an object of pity.

6. Be firm about holding the student to whatever academic and behavioral standards he or she is truly able to meet.

7. Do not isolate the student from activities. Recognize his or her need to participate in purposeful activity with peers.

Helping Children Through Death and Loss

When assisting a child to deal with death or loss, you should be:

- **Observant.** Determine what the child's understandings of death are.

- **Alert.** Pay attention to verbal and nonverbal communications.

- **Patient.** Important concerns may take time to rise to the surface.

- **Honest.** Truth is critical.

- **Attentive.** Shape responses to the individual, confirm what the individual has grasped.

- **Human.** Share your knowledge, experience, and reactions.

- **Supportive.** Continue to be available to the child.

Death Education

Children's feelings and thoughts regarding death are often ignored in our American culture. Frequently, children are not even told of the death of a significant other, because parents are struggling with their own grief and cannot believe that children would understand the tragic situation.

Teaching about death and dying tends to become more and more part of the curriculum at many levels of education from kindergarten to graduate school.

Children growing up today know about death. A pet is killed. Television features death in living color on the news and during prime time.

Death and dying conjure up different meanings to children than to adults. However, the facts of death should be explained to them naturally and lovingly. Flowers growing in the summer, then fading away in the fall and winter illustrate the sequencing of life and can help to explain that there are times for living things to grow and die. Traditional ways of explaining death, such as "mother has gone on a journey" or "God took dad because he was so good" or "Grandpa has gone to sleep" deny life's realities and cause children to have feelings of abandonment, betrayal and —later on— resentment.

Parents often wonder if children should go to funerals. There are no hard-and-fast rules and the opinions of experts vary. Some say that children over three should go. If funerals are a part of the family experience, then it seems appropriate. Any child who wishes to go to a funeral should go, if accompanied by an adult who can provide comfort and support. The child should be told beforehand, and in concrete terms, what will happen at the funeral.

The following are suggested goals in death education:

1. To inform the students of facts not currently widespread in the culture.
2. To help the student deal effectively with his or her own death and those of significant others.
3. To make the student an informed consumer of medical and funeral services.
4. To facilitate basic social changes through education.
5. To gain literary, philosophical, and artistic insights using death as a focus.

Stages of Grieving

In her book *On Death and Dying*, Elizabeth Kubler-Ross describes five states of dying, which a terminally ill patient goes through as part of a grieving process. They are:

1. Denial
2. Rage and Anger
3. Bargaining
4. Depression
5. Acceptance

Dr. Ross has also observed that persons close to the dying patient go through similar stages, but usually at a slower pace. The stages have become so widely known, that there is now a tendency to apply them almost too rigidly, with the assumption that everyone going through any kind of a grieving process must go through all five stages, in succession, or something is wrong. Dr. Ross herself cautions that the five stages are not absolute and that not everyone goes through each one in the same sequence. She recommends that they only be used in a flexible way as a tool to understand why a person who is grieving may behave in certain ways.

It is important for children to be included in mourning rituals — including the funeral — for someone with whom they have been emotionally close. If they are to resolve their feelings, children need to be allowed to express them — whether guilt, fear, or anger — with an accepting adult. Being "shielded" from the process (usually because it is assumed that it would be too much for them) might rob them of the opportunity to resolve their repressed feelings at the time when it is most appropriate to do so. Delayed reactions can result, and may be carried into adulthood.

Since children are not quick to verbally express their feelings about the loss of a loved one, they often displace their feelings on an external situation such as school. Therefore, it is important for school personnel to be alert to clues of emotional distress such as increased aggressiveness or apathy toward school work.

Facing Death: Six Stages

A person confronting impending death — that of self or another — must pass through six distinct stages. Depending on individual needs, the person may stay in one stage for a long time, move back and forth from one stage to another, or move from stage to stage following the sequence listed below.

Denial

This may be expressed by feeling nothing or insisting there has been no change. It is an important stage and gives people a 'time out" to reorganize. People in this stage need understanding and time.

Anger

Often, after denying a situation, people turn around and react. This reacting can be defined as anger. It can be expressed in nightmares and fears and in disruptive behavior. People in this stage need opportunities to express anger in a positive and healthy way.

Bargaining

The purpose of bargaining is to regain a loss. Consequently, a promise is made to do something in order to get something in return. Bargaining may be expressed through threats, tantrums or demands. It can also be expressed in angelic behavior or perfectionistic tendencies.

Depression

This sets in when it is realized that anger and bargaining will not work and one begins to understand that change may be permanent. This is the stage of grieving for whomever or whatever is lost. People in this stage need to know that others understand and are concerned about their feelings.

Acceptance

Acknowledgment of a death — a period of calm after release of emotions, demonstrated by a lifting of sadness and a willingness to keep living.

Hope

Evidenced by a revitalization of energy, a renewed interest in old friends, the development of new friendships, and the return of a sense of humor.

After a Death in the Family

The literature indicates that during childhood, one of every twenty children in the United States will lose a parent to death. By the age of 16, one of every five children will have lost at least one parent. If this exposure to death is extended by including the rest of the student's family and close relatives and friends, bereavements among students will occur at least a few times during each school year. Following are some suggestions for helping students face such losses.

1. Remember that adults can make a difference in helping students when they have problems with death, because most of them have faced the death of loved ones or other significant losses.

2. Listen and empathize. Also listen for what is NOT being said.

3. Maintain a sympathetic, never shaming, attitude toward the student's age-appropriate responses.

4. Respond with real feelings. The manner in which you express them is irrelevant.

5. Allow the student to cry by giving permission: "Go ahead and cry — it's all right." Permission may be necessary, since so many strong feelings are labeled as being publicly unacceptable and some students are taught to show only a stoical face in public.

6. Share personal experiences with death; mention things that helped others during such times. This helps to take away some of the loneliness a student feels.

7. Remember that ignoring grief does not cause it to go away. Research has indicated a relationship between antisocial behavior in adolescents and unresolved grief over the death of a loved one.

8. Assure younger children that having had negative feelings about the person at some time does not make them responsible for his or her death.

9. Be aware of what may be happening at home. Particularly during the early stages of grief, parents and siblings may experience physical illness, insomnia, severe depression, periods of crying, or illusions in which they see or hear the deceased.

10. Expect unusual behavior. Students may evidence an inability to concentrate on school work, an unusual amount of daydreaming, or a tendency to withdraw. Physiological reactions such as insomnia, nightmares, general nervousness, trembling, headaches, vomiting, and excessive appetite may accompany a student's attempts to deal with grief.

11. Refer students for help when necessary. This is a tricky area because sometimes normal grief looks very much like mental illness. When a teacher sees behaviors such as regressive changes in bowel and bladder control, persistent sleep problems, excessive aggression, hyperactivity, extended loss of concentration, extended withdrawal, continued regression into lower developmental behavior levels, wild swings in emotion, or thoughts that indicate a loss of contact with reality, it is time to refer that student.

12. Recognize that grief may last over an extended period of time. Where grief is openly and deeply expressed, the first six months constitute the most stressful period, with recovery beginning during the first year and occurring more conclusively by the end of the second year.

Subconcepts About Death That Children Attempt to Understand

- **Universality.** Does everyone die? Is death inevitable — does everyone have to die? Is death unpredictable—could it happen anytime?

- **Irreversibility.** Once the physical body of a living thing is dead, it can never be alive again.

- **Nonfunctionality.** Children may ask what bodies do when they are dead. One way to answer is to talk about what they *don't* do. "You don't laugh when you're dead." "You don't eat chocolate when you're dead."

- **Causality.** Questions include, "Why do people die?" "Do people die because they are bad?"

- **Continued life forms.** Children ask questions like, "What happens after death?" "Where does your soul go when you die?"

Developmental Responses to Death, Loss, and Grief

Understanding of death depends on many factors, including age, personality, level of maturity, previous experience with death, relationship to the person who died, and family background. The more you know about the individual child, the more you will be able to respond appropriately to his or her needs.

PRE-K - KINDERGARTEN

Children at this level may...
- see death as reversible, not final, and may expect the dead person to return.
- see death as accidental or incidental, not as something that happens to everyone.
- believe that his or her actions are responsible for death and may connect unrelated events. (Grandma died because I said I didn't like her.)
- think of death as living in another place.
- engage in wish fulfillment. (If I wish hard enough, Uncle Jo will come back.)

Children of this age may react by...
- showing anxiety about the possibility of their own death and the death of family members.
- asking when the dead person will return.
- responding intermittently to grief with a brief, strong reaction and then returning to normal activity, such as play, as a way of relieving stress.
- being confused or upset by the disruption in normal family routine and the grief of close family members and others.
- having normal fears heightened (fear of the dark, new places, going to sleep), and perhaps regressing to thumb-sucking or bed-wetting.
- crying easily or becoming angry about things that don't usually cause tears or anger.

(Continued Next Page)

GRADES 1-3

Children at this level may...

- begin to understand that death is final and irreversible, but may see death as happening only to some people, not to everyone.
- personify death as someone or something that sneaks up on people and takes them away.
- fear that death is contagious, something you catch like a cold.
- see themselves as responsible.
- be confused by words and euphemisms.

Children of this age may react by...

- being fearful of going to sleep or being separated from family members.
- showing physical symptoms such as fatigue or loss of appetite.
- trying to hide grief so as not to upset the family.
- asking for detailed explanations of why and how.
- engaging in symbolic play, such as playing "death," "burial," or "funeral."

GRADES 4-6

Children of this age may...

- understand that death is final and irreversible and begin to understand that it happens to everyone.
- have a heightened sense of their own fragility and vulnerability and a fear of bodily harm.
- think that death is punishment for bad behavior.
- feel guilty about their own thoughts.
- show curiosity about the physical and biological details of death.
- show concern about relationships and lifestyle changes. (Who will take care of Grandpa now that Grandma is dead? How will we have enough money without Dad? Will we have to move away?)

Children of this age may react by...

- having difficulty concentrating on schoolwork and activities.
- becoming withdrawn and isolated or angry and aggressive.
- trying to hide feelings — to protect family members or because they can't express feelings in ways they think others will understand.
- showing concern for "correct" behavior. (How should I act?)

SUICIDE

Facts about Suicide

Teenage suicides occur among all social classes, economic groups, races, and religions — even among those not thought to be obviously troubled.

Nationally, the number of reported adolescent suicides is on the rise.

Suicide is the third most common cause of death for youth ages 15 to 20, and the fourth leading cause of death in children ages 10 through 14.

The National Institute of Mental Health believes that as many as 25 suicides are attempted for each one that is completed. For every documented suicide, many go undetected and are registered as accidental deaths, notably fatal auto crashes.

Research indicates that adolescents from families in which suicide has occurred or which have a history of drug or alcohol abuse or depression are more at risk.

Suicide is different for males and females, attempted and completed suicides alike. Females attempt suicide more often than males, but males are four times more likely to die from suicide than females. Females are more likely to use drugs or cut their wrists – methods which allow them time to reconsider their actions. Males are more likely to use more fatal methods – firearms, hanging, or jumping from great heights. Sixty percent of all suicides in the U.S. make use of guns.

Most teens don't leave notes; 80% communicate their intentions verbally.

Little evidence indicates that talking about suicide actually "plants the idea" in the minds of adolescents.

The greatest teenage suicide risk factors include:

- Aggressive behavior
- Disruptive behavior
- Substance abuse
- Depression

Ninety percent of those who kill themselves actually have depression or other mental health issues.

The CDC reports that 60 percent of high-school students claim that they have thought about suicide and about 9 percent say they have attempted suicide.

The National Conference of State Legislatures (NCSL) reports that:

- 19.3% of high-school students have seriously considered suicide
- 14.5% of high-school students made actual plans

The American Association of Suicidology states that:

- Each year, there are approximately 10 youth suicides for every 100,000 youth
- Each day, there are approximately 12 youth suicides
- Every 2 hours and 11 minutes, a person under the age of 25 completes a suicide

Social Conditions Associated with Suicide

- family breakdowns, problems, and pressures
- communication breakdown with significant others where expressed depressed feelings are not acceptable
- feelings of isolation and loneliness — not being appreciated/ understood
- pressures to succeed without emotional support and/or coping skills (competitiveness with peers, demands from parents)
- academic failure
- increased availability of drugs or alcohol
- physical, psychological, or sexual abuse
- lack of structure in lives/ too much structure (persistent boredom)
- greater social freedom and fewer limitations
- disintegration of traditional system
- less spiritual commitment
- isolation in an increasingly mobile and rootless society
- depression, feelings of hopelessness, failure
- rejection from college
- breaking up of a close relationship
- family history of suicide and/or chronic depression

Making an Intervention

Many suicides can be averted. Even seriously suicidal people are torn between the wish to live and the wish to die. Often, it is not even death they are seeking, but relief from extreme, temporarily acute pain. Suicidal urges pass. Some people get through a crisis and never again seriously consider suicide.

If you are concerned that a young person is contemplating suicide, there are many things you can do to be of help, and some things you should try to avoid. Although the following paragraphs contain many suggestions, the main task for most people who work with youths is simply to have a qualified person assess the situation further.

Things to Do

Here is a summary of positive actions anyone can take to help prevent a suicide:

- If you are talking with the adolescent, stay calm and stay available. Do not panic. Stay with the suicidal person. If the person has called you on the phone, use another phone to call for help. Keep the adolescent on the line. If you have to hang up, make sure the adolescent gives you a phone number where he or she can be called back. Before hanging up, try to get not only the phone number but the exact location he or she is calling from. If another person and another phone are available, the call can be traced.

- Listen to what your feelings and intuition are telling you. If what you have seen and heard from a young person makes you think that there is a risk of suicide, act on that belief. Do not let others talk you out of taking positive action simply because they think you are overreacting.

- Call a trained professional for advice. Right now, *before* you encounter a suicidal youth, find out whom you should contact if and when a crisis arises: a student assistance counselor, administrator, agency psychologist, your agency in school, the staff of a mental health crisis unit, or a suicide prevention center. Do not wait for the crisis to occur. Be prepared.

- Tell people who need to know or who can help. Get significant others involved, especially parents or others who live with the person. When contacting others, keep the following points in mind:

You can give the youth an opportunity to participate in the decision as to whom to contact first. Several options can be presented, e.g., "Now that we both know how serious this is, we cannot just let it be a secret between you and me. We do need to include somebody else who can help. We can talk together about who that person might be." At this point, suggest the parents, a school social worker, a guidance counselor, or anyone else who can help start the process of intervention. This gives young people a sense that the process is not being taken entirely out of their hands and that they do have some control over the process. Regardless of whom they choose to contact first, of course, the parents must be notified quite soon after that.

When contacting parents, do not expect them to behave the way the young person thinks they will. It is not uncommon for depressed adolescents to believe their parents are uncaring or unconcerned when, in fact, they will express very strong concern for their children. Parents may also surprise the caller with some crucial information, such as a young person's past history of suicide threats and attempts or a recent family crisis that was not mentioned by the youth.

In the event that parents are unwilling to believe the situation is serious and unwilling to act, you may have to bolster your case by having someone else in the school or agency contact the parents to support what they have been told. In an emergency police may be needed to assist. Your district policies should be followed in this case. Contact your principal

- Even if one has already made general agreements about the privacy of individual or group counseling sessions, that confidence may be broken in the case of suicidal adolescents. Life-threatening situations are not included in agreements about the confidentiality of counseling, especially with minors. This is true even if such an exception was not made explicit beforehand.

- Assist the parents in getting help from a mental health professional .

- Follow through immediately and in the long run. Although competent parents will be able to guide their children to appropriate services, make sure that someone has continued to assist the youth after the initial contact. Getting a person to an emergency unit after an overdose of pills does not necessarily guarantee that useful services will be provided to help with the problems that led to the suicide attempt.

- Get support for yourself. Talk to a friend or colleague about the incident. Review what you did. Be open, talk about feelings of self-doubt and concerns for the suicidal youth.

Hints for Dealing with a Potential Suicide

- **Listen.** Allow the student to express feelings. Don't feel obligated to give advice or find simple solutions.
- **Be Honest.** Be in touch with your own feelings.
- **Share Feelings.** Allow your own humanity to show. Let the students know they are not alone and that feelings of depression and hopelessness do not last indefinitely.
- **Get help.** Contact parent/guardian and clearly urge contacting a mental health professional.
- **Make the call.** Contact the National Suicide Prevention Lifeline at (800) 273-talk (8255) for someone else or yourself.

Things Not To Do

Sometimes, even with the best of intentions and greatest degree of concern, our natural reactions to the fear and pain involved in working with suicidal youth can lead to unproductive attitudes and behaviors. If you are faced with suicidal youth, do not:

- Argue or debate with the person about the ethics, fairness, or morality of committing suicide.

- Pass judgment on the person, take offense, act appalled, or disappointed in the person.

- Ignore the signs or stop working with the person merely because he or she appears to be manipulative, whiney, extremely immature, or attention-seeking. People actually kill themselves in order to get attention. Even if a person appears to be using suicide threats to manipulate, it shows that suicide is on that person's mind.

- Make promises that are not in your power to keep, or give false assurances that everything will be all right.

- Assume that a recent attempt that has passed without serious consequences means the crisis is over.

- Abandon the person because the pain is too oppressive and burdensome. If it feels that way, get another trusted person in on the situation as soon as possible.

Determining the Degree of Risk

The first thing to be said about estimating the risk of suicide is: Don't do it before taking action. Act on your concerns, feelings, and intuition, and leave the assessment of suicide risk to psychologists, psychiatrists, clinical social workers, nurse clinicians, specially trained crisis-unit personnel, and other mental health professionals. Nevertheless, even though you may not be responsible for assessing or diagnosing potentially suicidal youth, being aware of the criteria will help confirm concerns whenever these signs are present.

Previous Threats. There is a big difference between having suicidal thoughts and making suicidal threats. If a person has mentioned to others that he or she is planning to commit suicide, that is a threat, and those who have threatened suicide are more likely to attempt suicide.

Previous Attempts. Any previous suicide attempts, whether they were life threatening or "suicidal gestures" increase the likelihood that a person will make an attempt in the future. Suicide gestures do not mean the person is not serious about dying. Many suicidal persons gradually escalate their attempts. In a suicide gesture, a person usually tells someone ahead of time, uses a less lethal means of self-harm (a low dose of aspirin as opposed to a gun, for instance) and takes steps to ensure discovery and rescue.

Specificity of Plan. A person who plans exactly how, when, and where he or she will attempt suicide is at higher risk than one who does not have a specific plan.

Availability of Means. A person who has the means, such as a gun or pills, to carry out suicide is at higher risk than one who does not.

How Lethal Are the Means? Threats to use a gun are more worrisome than a vague suggestion of overdosing on aspirin, for instance.

Lack of Rescue Resources. Sometimes no rescue resources are available because the person has planned to be isolated during the suicide attempt. Sometimes the person's general family situation accounts for this lack of resources, such as when one or both parents are away from home for business or vacations. Alcoholic parents are often unreliable rescue resources.

Accumulation of Signs and Stressors. The signs of depression, masked depression, and increased stress can be used not only to identify those who may be at risk, but also to estimate the extent of the risk. The more signs of depression and the more stress factors in a person's life, the more likely it is that suicide is a danger.

History of Suicide in the Family. The incidence of suicide in a person's family history increases the suicide risk for that person.

Gender. Boys are much more likely than girls to make serious suicide attempts. In general, females attempt suicide more frequently, but males complete suicide more frequently. Those who complete suicide are usually more active, aggressive, and impulsive than those who make an attempt but survive.

A Romanticized View of Suicide and Death. During the time immediately preceding a suicide attempt, the adolescent may go through a process of putting suicide in a positive or even glamorous light. "Death is going to be a beautiful thing," and "My parents will be better off when I'm gone," are thoughts frequently found in suicide notes. Some youths, when asked, will admit they get pleasure out of visualizing the attention they would get at their funerals.

Death Not Seen as Permanent. Some younger children do not grasp the concept that death is a permanent state. Those youths, as a consequence, do not fear the finality of death.

There are many different recommendations you can make when faced with a suicidal adolescent. In general, if the risk is high and available support — especially from the family and close friends — is not strong and reliable, hospitalization becomes more likely. If the young person has strong family support and appears to be calming down as a result of the immediate intervention by concerned adults, the youth might be sent home with the parents. In every case further counseling and support should be part of the discussion.

How to Deal with a Suicide

The suddenness, inscrutability, and increasing likelihood of suicide occurring in our communities is a concern to all. Given the sheer numbers of young people attempting and committing suicide today, it is clear that there is a need for a prepared, broad response to the problem.

Don't Play the Blame Game. One of the saddest outcomes of a suicide is the amount of anger, resentment, and finger-pointing that goes on. In communities where a number of suicides have taken place, it is not uncommon for school, social services, or church officials to call for a community meeting to help with the healing process. These meetings can easily degenerate into a battle over who is at fault for the suicide(s). Such arguments do little to help a community answer its questions and less to help prevent future suicide attempts.

It is not always helpful to get a "suicide expert" for these meetings. Experts' research or experience tends to address the specifics of adolescent depression and adolescent suicide rather than the communities reaction to tragedy. However, an unbiased, nonthreatening moderator who is respected by most people in the community can be helpful. This person can help to identify negative, destructive processes during such community meetings. He or she can help reframe accusations into less destructive statements. The moderator can also point out that anger and resentment are based on fear and a sense of helplessness rather than on any objective assessments of incompetence on the part of individual or agencies.

Counseling in the Wake of Suicide

Suicide is a tragedy. It is a response to pain. It signals total defeat and leaves devastation in its wake for family, friends, and community. In view of this, you will be dealing with a continuum of feelings. The following should be considered when discussing suicide with those who are left behind.

Feelings/Reactions

- Shock: slowed reaction, flat affect, hysteria
- Fear
- Anger
- Guilt
- Confusion
- Loss
- Disorientation
- Depression
- Sadness
- Discomfort

Educate the Media. There is a general consensus among mental health professionals that it can be destructive for the media to play youth suicide up in a sensational way. Recent experience has shown that suicide can be "contagious," that "copycat" suicides do take place.

It is best if the media know before a suicide takes place that the way they deal with a young person's death may have a direct effect on other youths in the community. The professional mental health community and school counselors who have worked with suicidal youth can attempt, both as individuals or members of task forces, to explain the problem of suicide contagion and suggest ways to decrease the likelihood of copycat suicides. If the media have not already been sensitized to this issue, someone — anyone available who can convince them of the need for caution — should talk to them during a crisis to try to get them to avoid a sensational approach.

The main point to get across to the media is to avoid glamorizing the suicide or suicide victim:

- Do not run the story on the front page of the newspaper. Try to limit coverage of the event to the obituary page.
- Keep stories short, but include enough facts to reduce conjecture and rumor.
- Do not run a picture of the deceased in the paper.
- Do not quote directly from the suicide note. Having last words printed in the paper is a fantasy that appeals to unstable or troubled youth. The most that should be run is a paraphrase of the contents of the suicide note.

These admonitions apply to school publications as well as community newspapers. Even though student editors might have been given much discretion regarding what they choose to print, they must be made aware of the possible effects that their coverage of a suicide might have. Effusive eulogies accompanied by a photograph of the suicide victim can be harmful. The editors and writers should consider these matters before publication.

The media have a positive role to play regarding suicide. They can be most helpful in countering teen suicide by featuring stories about the general social and emotional problems that lead to suicide.

An Action Plan for Schools

If any member of the school staff hears of a student's suicide, the first order of business is to contact the school administrator. The school administrator should oversee all subsequent school responses. Some steps that should be taken are:

- Contact the police, relatives, close friends of the family, or the parents to confirm the facts of the situation. All public information such as when and where the person was found, the sequence of events leading up to the suicide and other relevant details should be obtained. The family may not want people to know every detail but they should be told that the more facts known immediately about the suicide, the fewer rumors there will be later.

- All faculty should be notified immediately. If the news comes after school hours, some type of phone tree should be used to get the word to everyone. The purpose of the phone tree is to give staff members the basic information and to get them to a meeting before classes start on the next day of school. A phone tree, of course, should be in effect before a suicide or similar crisis occurs.

- Before the next day of school, all faculty should meet to learn the facts of the situation, to express their feelings about the event, to share concerns for the staff, students, and parents, and to hear about the plans to give information and counseling to students. It is important that all staff in the school learn the basic, simple facts of the case. If every student hears these facts during the first class period of the day, many rumors and misconceptions will be avoided.

INDICATORS OF POTENTIAL TEEN SUICIDES

High-Risk Indicators

- Suicide attempts known by significant other
- Family history of suicide
- Distributes favorite belongings to special friends or family members
- Extreme grief or trauma experienced due to tragic loss (e.g.., death, suicide, divorce, separation, change in family status or residence, negative change in health status or appearance)
- When questioned, expresses wish to die and indicates plan, available means and specific time-frame for completion
- Drugs, including alcohol, used excessively
- Involved in high-risk activities
- Evidences careless disregard for personal safety
- Scratches and marks body

Other General Indicators

- Verbalizing suicide threats
- Collecting information on suicide methods
- Expressing hopelessness, helplessness or anger at self or world
- Expresses death or depression themes
- Evidences physical symptoms of depression
- Makes comments such as, "I don't want to live any longer," and "You'll be better off without me"
- Expresses that friend and family will not miss them
- Threatens to hurt or kill self
- Makes inquiries regarding lethal weapons, pills and other methods used by people who have committed suicide
- Expresses that no one cares
- Conversation, written expression, reading selections and art work focus on death and other morbid subjects

Direct Actions for Preventing Suicide

If detailed plans have been made and the means of suicide obtained, the danger is great. Do not ignore the issue. The following actions are advisable:

1. **Offer support, understanding and compassion.**

2. **Confront the problem openly.** Be direct, do not be afraid to discuss suicide with the student. Do not make moral judgments. Getting the student to talk about it is a positive step. It will be necessary to spend sufficient time allowing the individual to vent feelings before trying to cope with or solve the problem.

3. **Be affirmative and supportive.** Isolation is one of the worst conditions for someone who is suicidal.

4. **Contact the parents.** Parents should be informed of your concern. A school employee is not held liable for breach of confidence for taking action on behalf of students whose behavior may be inimical to themselves or others. The student should be released only to a parent or someone who can provide help.

5. **Encourage professional help.** Contact should be made with a suicide prevention center, mental health clinic, or other appropriate agency. Make the parent aware of the sources of help. Initiate the contact with the appropriate agency.

6. **Affirm dignity and worth.** In all your dealings with suicidal students, do everything possible to preserve their dignity, self-worth and sense of personal value. By building them up, you will help them overcome the need to tear themselves down.

7. **Keep a record of the contacts.** Summarize all interactions with the suicidal student. File a report according to the policy of the school.

NATURAL DISASTERS

Following a hurricane, tornado, fire, earthquake, or any other form of natural disaster, you will be dealing with individuals who have just experienced a severe incident over which they felt powerless. The resulting stress and strain will be unusually high. Most of the reactions will be similar to those common to victims of other traumatic events: shock, disbelief, guilt, and anger.

One significant difference is that typically many more people are directly affected by a natural disaster. This can generate a feeling of mutual support and camaraderie which may never before have existed in the same group of people.

Expect media coverage to be widespread, and to result in numerous outside attempts to render assistance. The curious will abound, and profit seekers may attempt to gain financially from the misfortune of victims. After recovering from the initial shock of the incident and the grief associated with personal and material losses, the victims may feel overwhelmed by the attention they are receiving from so many strangers, and may be unable to differentiate between genuine offers of assistance and curiosity or profit-seekers. In response to all of this, some may simply wish to be left alone. These feelings should be respected while you are providing psychological first aid.

Feelings/Reactions

- Helplessness
- Fear
- Fight or Flight Syndrome
- Immobility
- Nonverbal Hysterics
- Pointless Physical Activity
- Confusion

Dealing with the Feelings/Reactions

- Convey that you want to understand how the victim feels.
- Apply gentle firmness and kindness.
- Allow the victim to talk freely for a brief time.
- Convey information through facial expressions and gestures, as well as words.
- Maintain patience.
- Assign tasks.
- Suggest simple, routine jobs that victims can perform.
- Accept handicaps.
- Help rediscover quickly a few skills/abilities that the victim can use at once.

- Share a few words of encouragement.
- Find out if the victim has concerns about family/friends. Give information regarding where/how the victim may be able to make contact.
- Give factual, up-to-date information.
- Be warmly interested and kind, not overly sympathetic.
- Dissuade the victim from voicing destructive ideas. Redirect energies toward useful pursuits.

Physical Side Effects

- Trembling
- Rapid breathing
- Shortness of breath
- Rapid pulse
- Excessive perspiration
- Crying
- Weakness
- Nausea
- Vomiting
- Self-centeredness
- Blindness to reality
- Atoning for past mistakes
- Scapegoating
- Anger

Things to Keep in Mind

1. Cultural/ethnic/gender differences in reaction
2. Religious convictions
3. Feelings expressed are real, not to be denied or ignored
4. Residual issues may arise — post-traumatic stress syndrome
5. Media presence
6. Make a reasonably candid appraisal of your strengths and limitations
7. Remember that responses will be individualized. Don't expect everyone to go through the same stages.

First Aid Strategies: Natural Disasters

Children and adults need facts. Give a realistic orientation of what the particular disaster is (earthquake, hurricane, etc.) — how and when it happens. Prepare students for the probability that other events related to the primary disaster may well occur (aftershocks, fire, civil unrest, etc.). Remind students that only certain areas may have been affected.

Children and adults need opportunities to share feelings and experiences. Talking helps diminish anxieties. Adults need to admit their own feelings so children will have "permission" to share theirs. This is especially true with older boys. Have the students draw "what the particular disaster looks like." Then ask them to describe their pictures. Activities like this help elicit feelings.

Children fear separation from family members. Children are not as fearful of their own personal safety as they are of being separated from their parents and not knowing if their loved ones are safe or will see them again. If the disaster is one that occurs suddenly and/or without warning, let students know that parents will get to them as soon as they are able. In the meantime, assure students they will be cared for. Implement a buddy system with classmates. DO NOT LEAVE CHILDREN ALONE.

Engage children in activities. Activities are important to help gain some control over the situation. For example, in the case of an earthquake encourage students to straighten up the room and rearrange furniture and equipment for greater safety during aftershocks. Use classroom materials and recreational games to structure time.

Fear and Anxiety

Fear is a normal reaction to any danger that threatens life or well-being. After a disaster, children may be afraid of:

- recurrence of the event
- injury or death
- separation from family
- being left alone

Parents may ignore the emotional needs of their children once they are assured that nothing "serious" has happened to the family. Help them realize that their children may be very frightened. Help them understand the kinds of fear and anxiety a child experiences.

Advice to Parents

- Keep the family together.
- Reassure children with words as well as actions.
- Listen to what your children tell you about their fears.
- Listen when children tell you about how they feel and what they think about the disaster.
- Explain as much as you can concerning the facts of the disaster.
- As much as possible, continue to observe valued family routines and activities.

WAR

When Parents Are Deployed to a War Zone

When large numbers of military personnel are sent to a war zone, we can best serve our affected students by being proactive in providing a supportive learning environment which recognizes the issues of sudden deployment and the possibility of military conflict. Through engaging students in activities which open communication and provide information, we can prevent many possible behavioral problems, and ease those behaviors which exist.

Familiarize yourself with the symptoms of children in crisis, including: anxiety, distractibility, withdrawal, acting out, low motivation and failure to complete work. Keep at hand a current list of community resources that deal with deployment issues. Call appropriate groups when you have questions or need additional information.

In the classroom, provide learning activities that will assist student adjustment and promote peer support. Such activities might include:

- Determine which of your students have deployed parents, relatives, or friends. Discuss the normal emotions that often occur in families faced with sudden deployment. Allow students to share their own feelings. Provide an environment where students with deployed parents feel a sense of support from you and their classmates. Don't hesitate to discuss the pride that we as U.S. citizens have in our military personnel.

- Deal with the issue of prejudice before problems arise. It is important that students not generalize attitudes toward opponents in a military action to people of the same nationality, religion or ethnic decent who live in this country.

- Ask teachers to teach social studies and geography lessons based on the War Zone. They can focus on the location, weather, customs, and political issues, including reasons for the current conflict.

- Communicate with deployed parents or armed forces in general. Send letters, drawings, and other student work. This can reduce anxieties and allows students to feel involved and helpful.

The following are responses that can be experienced by children whose parent(s) is deployed:

Preschool & Kindergarten

Somatic Reactions:
- Loss of appetite
- Overeating
- Indigestion
- Vomiting

- Bowel or bladder problems (e.g. diarrhea, constipation, loss of sphincter control)
- Sleep disturbances and nightmares

Emotional/Behavior Reactions:
- Generalized fear (darkness, strangers, monsters)
- Regressive symptoms (thumb sucking, bed wetting, immature speech)
- Repetitive play in which the traumatic event is reenacted
- Appears helpless and passive
- Repetitive talking about experience or lack of verbalization
- Short attention span
- Irritability
- Overactiveness
- Exhibits anxious attachments such as clinging, not wanting to be away from parents
- Demonstrates cognitive confusion (does not understand the danger is over)
- Develops anxieties related to incomplete understanding about death; fantasizes about repairing the situation

Suggested First Aid:
- Provide physical comfort such as food, rest, holding, soothing bedtime routine
- Assure adult protection
- Give repeated concrete clarifications of events
- Encourage communication with teachers and parents

- Provide help in verbalizing general feelings and complaints
- Explain the physical reality of death

Elementary School

Somatic Reactions:
- Headaches
- Complaints of visual or hearing problems
- Persistent itching and scratching
- Nausea
- Sleep disturbances, nightmares, night terrors

Emotional/Behavior Reactions:
- Inability to concentrate, drop in level of school achievement
- Irritability
- Aggressive behavior
- Disobedience
- Sadness over loss of possessions
- Regressive reactions (excessive need for adult's attention, clinging, crying, whimpering)
- Resistance to going to school
- Preoccupation with own actions during event as they relate to responsibility and guilt
- Retells and replays the event; distorts the event cognitively; obsessively details the event
- Is concerned about own safety and safety of others such as siblings

- Is afraid of feelings (afraid to cry, to be angry)
- Is concerned for other victims and their families

Suggested First Aid
- Reassure with realistic information
- Permit acting out of experience
- Acknowledge the normalcy of the feelings
- Temporarily lessen requirements for optimum performance in school and home
- Encourage verbal expression of thought and feelings about disaster/loss
- Provide opportunity for structured but not demanding chores and responsibilities
- Encourage physical activity
- Give older children useful tasks to perform
- Encourage constructive activities on behalf of the injured or deceased

VIOLENCE & GANG DISTURBANCES

Dealing with violence requires an attitude and demeanor of calmness, reason, and self-control.

Establish protocol for handling violent situations. An assault can occur at any time anywhere in the school, so guidelines should be mindful of where such incidents may take place (in the classroom or parking lot, for instance), at what time of day (before or after school or during class), and against which staff (teachers, office staff, volunteers). In business, this type of planning is called a "threat assessment."

Decide what staff should and should not do if assaulted, where they should flee, and whom they should notify. Train school staff in self-defense and verbal de-escalation techniques.

Things to Keep in Mind

- Cultural/ethnic/gender differences
- Periodically reassess to maintain an overall awareness of the situation and emotional climate.
- Maintain a non-challenging yet professionally secure attitude.

- Consider personal safety issues.
- Know how to recognize individual gangs.
- Know what territories the gangs claim.
- Separate gang members, particularly the members at odds.
- Coordinate your activities with the police, if they are involved.
- Translators may be needed.

Feelings/Reactions	Hints for Dealing with Them
Anger	Allow to vent briefly. Remain calm.
Anxiety	Demonstrate empathy.
Fear	Listen. Assess safety concerns.
Grief	Allow to experience. Provide support system if warranted.
Hysteria	Remain patient. Isolate if necessary.
Physical injury	Share a few words of encouragement. Maintain medical support.
Pride over reaction	Allow to express briefly, then refocus toward resolution.
Revenge	Maintain non judgmental attitude. Be alert regarding plans to retaliate. Promote resources such as mediation, use of school or community authorities to resolve issues, as alternatives to retaliation.
Rumors	Give accurate, up-to-date information that might defuse rumor.

KIDNAPPING/ABDUCTION

Kidnapping may be committed by strangers, as well as a non-custodial parent.

Feelings/General Reactions

- Fear
- Disbelief, panic, denial, anger, sadness
- Guilt
- Unrealistic expectations of one's capabilities
- "This can't happen to me" syndrome
- Helplessness
- Confusion
- Paranoia
- Naivete

Prevention Strategies

- Reassure students that they can be smart and resourceful in a potentially dangerous situation.
- Caution students that the behavior and attitude of strangers can initially be friendly, yet terrifying.

- Allow students to tell you their "success" stories of how they managed in similar situations.
- In a simple, straightforward way, alert students to the common verbal "come-ons" of strangers.
- Give students permission to say "no" to strangers — to be unfriendly.

Issues and Points to Keep in Mind

1. Abduction laws differ from state to state. The range extends from misdemeanor to felony.
2. Feelings expressed are real, not to be denied or discounted.
3. Residual effects may surface.
4. Media presence and its impact.
5. Personal, candid appraisal of self.

Helpful Resource

Child Quest International is dedicated to the prevention and recovery of missing, abused, and exploited children. They provide prevention education, safety information and programs, as well as support for left-behind families.

www.childquest.org

contact: (408) 287-4673

sightings: (888) 818-4673

TERRORIST/HOSTAGE SITUATIONS

A trained outside agency needs to be contacted immediately. There are different kinds of hostage-takers: suicidal types, parents using children as a way to get to the other parent, true psychotics, and terrorists. A usable generality is that anyone who takes hostages has a great desire for something and cannot see any other way to get it. *The job of the negotiator is to find out what the hostage-taker wants and help find an alternative way to get it.* It is important to help him or her understand that the hostages are only valuable alive and healthy, but it is also important not to communicate too much value on the hostages.

Normally, hostage situations will be handled by law enforcement authorities, but crisis counselors should have some familiarity with how to deal with a hostage situation if the need should arise. Since the administrator is initially the decision maker at a school, that person would probably be in a better position to do the negotiating. If the decision maker isn't in direct negotiations, the negotiator can act as an intermediary between the hostage-taker and the authorities. This tends to defuse the threats a hostage taker might be able to exercise in direct negotiations with a decision maker.

Feelings/Reactions and Hints for Dealing with Them

Beginning of incident: Hostage taker will have high anxiety, an intense focus on his purpose. He will be sensitive and dangerous at this time.

1. Calmly ask for information on needs, without placing high value on hostages.

2. Keep hostage taker and hostages contained.

3. Establish a communications link (telephone if possible).

4. Turn off electricity and ventilation. It can be negotiated back on.

5. Gather any information on hostages and hostage-taker which is available from school records, etc.

After first half hour: Anxiety and bodily functions take over — need for elimination, water, and food. The hostage taker will start to see the hostages as people.

1. Keep discussing things with the hostage-taker. The purpose is to keep him calm.

2. Be willing to discuss anything, but require a price for what you give.

3. Don't trust hostages to give you accurate information while still being held.

Things to Keep in Mind

1. Since negotiation strategies have been developed, most have been successful.

2. You will probably be relieved by a law enforcement negotiator within one hour.

3. It may be necessary to counsel with family members of hostages. Explain to them how the process works and that the chances of success after the first half hour are very good. Avoid direct interaction between family members and hostage takers.

4. The media will usually be a factor.

5. After their release, hostages will need counseling. Depending on how long they have been held, they may have a wide range of emotions. One emotion that they may need to deal with is a sense of guilt or conflict over positive feelings they may have developed toward the hostage-taker. This is known as the Stockholm Syndrome and seems to be a common reaction.

HOW PARENTS CAN HELP IN A CRISIS

Much of the recovery work involving a crisis can best be facilitated by parents. If possible, the school should meet with parents in small groups and provide information as to what to look for and how they can help their children. Some parents may need individual help before they are ready to help their children.

In addition, provide opportunities for parents to discuss, in groups, their own responses and worries. Furnish materials to parents explaining normal childhood reactions to crisis situations, and how they (parents) can help.

Following a Crisis, Some Children May:

- become more active and restless.
- If homes have been damaged, worry where they will live and what will happen to them.
- become upset easily — crying and whining.
- be quiet and withdrawn, not wanting to talk about the experience.

- feel neglected by parents who are busy trying to clean up and rebuild their lives.
- become afraid of loud noises, rain, storms, etc.
- be angry, hit, throw and kick to show their anger, often with little provocation.
- be afraid to be left alone or afraid to sleep alone. They may have nightmares and want to sleep with a parent or another person.
- behave as they did when younger. They may start sucking their thumb, wetting the bed, asking for a bottle, wanting to be held.
- have symptoms of illness such as nausea, vomiting, headaches, fever, loss of appetite.
- be upset at the loss of a favorite toy, blanket, teddy bear, etc.
- feel guilty that they caused the disaster because of some previous behavior.
- refuse to go to school or to child care arrangements. The child may not want to be out of your sight.
- be afraid that the crisis may recur, especially if conditions recur, e.g., rain after a flood or aftershocks after an earthquake. They may ask many times, "Will it come again?"
- Not show any outward signs until weeks or months later.

Ways Parents Can Help Their Children

- Talk with your children, providing simple accurate information and answers to questions. Allow them to tell their stories about what happened.

- Talk with your children about your own feelings.

- Listen to what your children say and how they say it. Repeating your children's words, recognizing fear, anxiety and insecurity is very helpful. For instance: "You are afraid that . . ." or, "You wonder if the storm will come again today." This helps both you and your children clarify feelings.

- Reassure your child: "We are together." "We care about you." "We will take care of YOU."

- Respond to repeated questions. You may need to repeat information and reassurances many times.

- Hold the child. Provide comfort. Touching is important for children during this period.

- Spend extra time putting your child to bed. Talk and offer assurance. Leave night light on if necessary.

- Observe your child at play. Listen to what is said and how the child plays. Frequently children express feelings of fear or anger while playing with dolls, trucks or friends.

- Provide play experiences to relieve tension. Work with playdough, paint, play in water; given them something safe, like a pillow, ball or balloon.

- Allow children to mourn and grieve if they lose a meaningful toy or blanket. In time, it may be helpful to replace the lost object.

FORMS AND SAMPLE LETTERS

Sample
DOCUMENTATION LOG DURING A CRISIS SITUATION

Time	Chronological Listing of Events (Factual Information)	Comments/Results
11:03	Student was hit by a car in front of the school. Driver did not stop. Only first part of license was reported by Sara Smith — student patrol (2 FOB). Nurse on scene.	
11:04	911 called	
11:05	Students in front of school sent back to classrooms with teachers. Custodian rerouting traffic.	Many students crying.
11:06	CPR continuing — school nurse.	
11:09	Fire truck arrives. Life Flight called.	
11:11	District Crisis Response Team called	
11:12	Parents called	No answer.
11:14	Tried to contact father at work. Left message to call school.	
11:17	Called emergency number listed on card. Grandmother answered	She was told the school needed to locate mother but not that her grandson was seriously injured.
11:21	Life Flight arrived.	
11:22	District Crisis Team arrives.	
11:25	Reporters arrive.	Referred to principal.

DOCUMENTATION LOG DURING A CRISIS SITUATION

Time	Chronological Listing of Events (Factual Information)	Comments/Results

CRISIS SUMMARY REPORT

Date _____ School _____

District Personnel Involved: _____
_____

Brief Description of Incident: _____
_____
_____
_____
_____
_____
_____

Note: Attach copy of completed "Documentation Log" During a Traumatic Situation.

What Worked Well: _____
_____
_____
_____

Comments: _____
_____
_____
_____
_____

Need to Change for Future Response to Traumatic Events: _____
_____
_____
_____

SAMPLE STATEMENT FOR ANNOUNCEMENT OF CRISIS SITUATION

The following is a prototype script for the initial announcement concerning an emergency or crisis situation. It may be duplicated and distributed to teachers, and then read by teachers in the classroom, or it may be delivered by the principal or designee over the public address system to the entire school.

To:

From:

"We have just been advised of a tragedy involving a member of our school. It greatly saddens me to announce that _____ has died (has been in a serious accident). As soon as we have more information, we will pass it on to you. Members of the crisis response team will be available in the building to help anyone who needs extra support in dealing with this news. Your teachers will tell you the locations where you can receive support and the times it will be available.

"As soon as we know the family's wishes regarding _____, we will pass that information along to you. We ask that all students remain in their classrooms and adhere to their regular schedules."

SAMPLE BULLETIN TO PARENTS

SPECIAL BULLETIN

April 26, 2012

Dear Parents:

A suspicious telephone call was made to the school today. In order to ensure the safety of all students, the police were informed and the building evacuated and searched. Fortunately, it turned out to be a false alarm.

After consulting with the police, we have been informed that when a threat like this is made, there is rarely any actual danger.

If your child has any concerns, we will have the guidance counselor speak with him or her tomorrow.

Sincerely,

Sara Smith

Principal

SAMPLE LETTER TO PARENTS

Dear Parents

As you know, a tragedy occurred Saturday at Windy Hill Apartments. A student from our school was injured in a shooting and the families of a number of other students were directly or indirectly involved.

Tragedies like this can cause many different emotional reactions. Your children (and you) may be experiencing feelings like shock, fear, anger, hurt, sadness or confusion. As a parent, you may not be sure what to say or do to help your children through this difficult time. I hope that the following suggestions will be of assistance to you:

1. You child needs you now. Be there for him or her.

2. Let your children talk, write, or draw about their feelings.

3. An event like this can cause a child to recall past feelings about the deaths of family members or friends. Allow your child to express these feelings freely — time and time again.

4. You child may express the fear that you or other family members will die. That's a very realistic fear. Assure you child that you are there for him or her.

5. Death and dying conjure up different meanings to children than to adults. However, the facts of death should be explained to children naturally and lovingly.

6. Let children know that it's okay to experience anger, hurt, guilt, sadness — and that sometimes these feelings overlap. Also, it is really okay for your children to see you cry.

7. The behavior of your children may change temporarily. For example, they may become more restless, have trouble sleeping, act more hostile or more withdrawn.

The most important thing to remember is to be there for your children. Be gentle, understanding and, *above all*, just listen.

A crisis team from the district was at the school today to speak with students and staff affected by this tragedy. This team is available to any student or community member who would like support. Please feel free to contact the school office if you have any questions and/or concerns about this event or your child's well-being.

Sincerely,

Sara Smith
Principal

SAMPLE LETTER TO PARENTS

Dear Parents

As you know, a terrible tragedy occurred in front of our school yesterday, Tuesday, March 6, 2012. A kindergarten student was hit by a moving vehicle and later died at the hospital.

Events like this can cause many different emotional reactions. Your children (and you) may be experiencing feelings like shock, fear, anger, hurt, sadness or confusion. As a parent, you may not be sure what to say or do to help your children through this difficult time. I hope that the following suggestions will be of assistance to you:

1. You child needs you now. Be there for him or her.

2. Let your children talk, write, or draw about their feelings.

3. An event like this can cause a child to recall past feelings about the deaths of family members or friends. Allow your child to express these feelings freely — time and time again.

4. You child may express the fear that you or other family members will die. That's a very realistic fear. Assure you child that you are there for him or her.

5. Death and dying conjure up different meanings to children than to adults. However, the facts of death should be explained to children naturally and lovingly.

6. Let children know that it's okay to experience anger, hurt, guilt, sadness — and that sometimes these feelings overlap. Also, it is really okay for your children to see you cry.

7. The behavior of your children may change temporarily. For example, they may become more restless, have trouble sleeping, act more hostile or more withdrawn.

The most important thing to remember is to be there for your children. Be gentle, understanding and, *above all*, just listen.

We have support staff available at school, and through the school district office, to help you and your child should you need extra support. Call (phone number) to receive assistance.

Also, if you or your child wishes to send a note or card to the family of the victim, you may do so through the school. Or you may contribute to a trust fund which has been set up for the family. Send your donation to:

Trust Fund in memory of Bobby Smith
c/o (name and address)

SAMPLE GUIDELINES FOR PARENTS

Following a crisis some children may:

- Become more active and restless.
- If homes have been damaged, worry where they will live and what will happen to them.
- Become upset easily — crying and whining.
- Be quiet and withdrawn, not wanting to talk about the experience.
- Feel neglected by parents who are busy trying to clean up and rebuild their lives.
- Become afraid of loud noises, rain storms, etc.
- Be angry, hit, throw and kick to show their anger, often with little provocation.
- Be afraid to be left alone or afraid to sleep alone. They may have nightmares and want to sleep with a parent or another person.
- Behave as they did when they were younger. They may start sucking their thumb, wetting the bed, asking for a bottle, wanting to be held.
- Have symptoms of illness such as nausea, vomiting, headaches, or a fever. They may not want to eat.
- Be upset at the loss of a favorite toy, blanket, teddy bear, etc.
- Feel guilty that they caused the disaster because of some previous behavior.
- Refuse to go to school or to child care arrangements. They may not want to be out of your sight.
- Be afraid that the crisis may recur, especially if conditions recur, e.g., rain after a flood or after-shocks after an earthquake. They may ask many times, "Will it come again?"
- Not show any outward signs until weeks or months later.

SAMPLE GUIDELINES FOR PARENTS

Much of the recovery work following a crisis can best be facilitated by parents. If possible, meet with parents at school and provide information as to what to look for and how they can help their children.

Some parents may need assistance themselves before they are ready to help their children. If possible, provide opportunities for parents to discuss, in small groups, their own responses and worries. Materials such as the explanation below and the list of suggestions on the next page may be provided to parents.

YOUR CHILD NEEDS YOU

You have recently experienced a crisis in your lives. Family routines have been disrupted. You have much to do. As parents of a young child or children, you face tasks that are difficult and demanding.

A crisis affects the members of a family or an entire community. You may be immediately involved or have friends or neighbors who are affected. Likewise, your children may have friends who are involved.

It is hard for young children to understand what has happened to their home and family. Some may have completely mixed-up views of the situation, while others, depending on age and how they experienced the disaster, need your continued guidance and understanding to help them grow through the experience. How you help your child to work through this difficult time may have a lasting effect.

Children can experience the same intense feelings that you feel about the crisis. These are normal reactions. Each child in a family may react differently. Some children show their feelings in a direct and immediate fashion, others wait until a later time. Most children will be confused by the sudden interruption to their routine. This is a very difficult time for them, as well as you.

SAMPLE GUIDELINES FOR PARENTS

WAYS PARENTS CAN HELP THEIR CHILDREN

- Talk with your children, providing simple accurate answers to questions. Allow them to tell their stories about what happened.

- Talk with your children about your own feelings.

- Listen to what your children say and how they say it. It is very helpful to repeat your children's words, while recognizing fear, anxiety, insecurity and other feelings. For instance: "You are afraid that..." or "You're worried that the storm will come again today." This helps both you and your children clarify feelings.

- Reassure your child: "We are together." "We care about you." "We will take care of you."

- Respond to repeated questions. You may need to repeat information and reassurances many times.

- Hold your child. Provide comfort. Touching is important for children during this period.

- Spend extra time putting your child to bed. Talk and offer assurance. Leave a night light on if necessary.

- Observe your child at play. Listen to what is said and how the child plays. Frequently children express feelings of fear and anger while playing with dolls, trucks or friends.

- Provide play experiences to relieve tension. Work with playdough, paint, or play in water. Give them something safe to play with, like a pillow, ball, or balloon.

- Allow children to mourn and grieve if they lost a meaningful toy or blanket. In time, it may be helpful to replace the lost object.

ABOUT THE AUTHORS

Virginia Vanderway

Although Ginny Vanderway has held many and varied positions in education she is most fond of her years as a counselor and administrator with Student Support Services in the Cajon Valley School District. She has served on advisory boards for School Counseling programs at San Diego State University and University of San Diego. Currently, Ginny is a Fieldwork Supervisor for counseling interns at the University of San Diego.

Ginny was born in Buffalo, NY and received her Bachelor's and Master's Degrees from San Diego State University. She has two adult children and two grandchildren and lives in San Diego, California.

Carol Clarke

Carol taught at both elementary and middle school in the Cajon Valley Union School District before she became a middle school counselor. She has served on advisory boards for School Counseling programs at San Diego State University and University of San Diego. Currently, she is a Fieldwork Supervisor for counseling interns at the University of San Diego.

Carol was born in New York City, moved to San Diego during high school. She received her Bachelor's and Master's Degrees from San Diego State University. She has one grown son and now lives in Lakeside, California.

If your heart is in Social-Emotional Learning, visit us online.

Come see us at
www.InnerchoicePublishing.com

Our web site gives you a look at all our other Social-Emotional Learning-based books, free activities, articles, research, and learning and teaching strategies. Every week you'll get a new Sharing Circle topic and lesson.

INNERCHOICE Publishing
15079 Oak Chase Court
Wellington, FL 33414

www.ingramcontent.com/pod-product-compliance
Lightning Source LLC
Chambersburg PA
CBHW080551170426
43195CB00016B/2754